BINDWEED

First published in 2017 by
The Dedalus Press
13 Moyclare Road
Baldoyle
Dublin D13 K1C2
Ireland

www.**dedaluspress**.com

ISBN 978 1 910251 24 9

Dedalus Press titles are represented in the UK by
Inpress Books, www.inpressbooks.co.uk,
and in North America by Syracuse University Press, Inc.,
www.syracuseuniversitypress.syr.edu.

Cover image: 'Bindweed, Calestegia sepium'
by Aislinn Adams. By permission.
www.aislinnadams.com

The Dedalus Press receives financial assistance from
The Arts Council / An Chomhairle Ealaíon.

BINDWEED

MARK ROPER

for Catherine
with warmest wishes
Mark   October 2017

DEDALUS PRESS

ACKNOWLEDGEMENTS

Thanks are due to the editors of the following, in which some of these poems, or earlier versions of them, first appeared: *Abridged; American, British and Canadian Studies; Bank Street Postcard Poems; Birds & People,* Mark Cocker; *College Green; Even The Daybreak,* ed. Jessie Lendennie; *I Live In Michael Hartnett,* ed. James Lawlor; *Poetry Ireland Review; Poetry Salzburg Review; Temenos; The Goose; The Irish Times; The North; The Stony Thursday Book* and *What We Found There,* ed. Theo Dorgan.

Some of the poems have been broadcast on RTÉ Radio 1's *Sunday Miscellany.*

A bursary from The Arts Council and an award from The Society of Authors are gratefully acknowledged.

Special thanks to James Harpur and Grace Wells.

for Jane

CONTENTS

⌇

— 1 —

— 2 —

1

Longtailed Tits

A soft settling, sift of whisper, chink
and chitter and you're in the middle

of urgent conversation, six or seven
or eight or nine or ten of them talking

all at once *listen to me no you listen to me
no you listen no you* a carry-on hidden

in trees a speaking of leaves is it
a house of sound a second skin

a desperate *I'm here but where are you,*
birds vague in colour, light as dust,

so small they'd soon get lost in silence,
slip through cracks in the day, it's all

around you now tiny travelling circus
you're hanging on every word afraid

you'll miss something then it's gone
and you're hurrying after you're calling

*wait, I didn't catch that, what did you say,
sorry, don't mean to be rude, it was just that*

Moon

Battered companion,
your face a map of hurt
no tear consoles.

Closest friend,
it would be so much harder
without you.

You come and go,
punchdrunk,
proud of your scars.

Always ready
for one more round,
wanting the night

never to end.
Golden bowl,
no matter how broken.

Shadow

Skittish as a foal
when light lets you out,
lashed to my feet
but free of my feeling.

Loved by the moon,
sharpened to a blade,
stretched a hundred feet,
shrunk to a stub.

The same but separate.
Always ready to do
something I don't.
Troubling double,

your face hidden,
back always turned,
your dark matter
neither life nor soul.

Rearing up to frighten
on a firelit wall.
Raising questions
that go unanswered.

The Wader Cabinet

(NATURAL HISTORY MUSEUM, DUBLIN)

Fleshings of weather and estuary,
plumage a wash of mud, stone and silver.

Darners of shoreline, beaks' quick needles
mending and mending the fraying edges.

Calls the haunt and hallow of marshland.
Eyes wired to wind and tide, mile-watchful.

Careers of risk and rapidity cut short
they suffer our stare in this cabinet,

as if by a closer look we might learn
how best to let them keep their distance.

Among them here an eskimo curlew,
a last likeness, a bird extinct –

whatever we might have promised, denied,
whatever might have bound us, untied.

Curlew Sandpiper

(NATURAL HISTORY MUSEUM, DUBLIN)

i.m. Michael Hartnett

Head aslant,
at work
and wary,

thin beak
all instinct
and grip,

one eye
hard to
the ground,

one eye
sharp
for departure.

Anglewise,
quick-witted
wings

pinned
to a split
second –

still a startle
to see it
so still.

Great Northern Diver

(NATURAL HISTORY MUSEUM, DUBLIN)

I know you from the Rinnashark,
a single, solemn, heavy bird,
eking out brief winter days in silence,
an ashy skulker in a channel.

A ghost of the shining example
by the door in the Dead Zoo:
a male bright in the summer plumage
we shouldn't see, colours that ripen

like a night sky when you leave to breed
on a lonely American lake,
black back stamped with star,
white stone strung round throat.

In its cabinet rising to the occasion,
looking down on lesser divers
to either side, lording it over petrel,
razorbill, shearwater and guillemot.

Rising from the past with shoals of skin
and herds of fur, red deer all air and bone,
half-creatures here to greet us
from a land between life and death.

Watching small feet wear out the tiles,
listening to children chant as they go:
Bye Otters, Bye Hares, Bye Sun Fish, Bye Whale,
Bye-bye Badger, Bye-bye Diver, Bye-bye Seal.

Carving

A European Bison, sculpted from a mammoth tusk,
some 22,000 years old, found in Zaraysk, Russia, in 2001

Hump of muscled shoulder
moulded from the tusk's taper.

Horn and ear picked cleanly out,
nostrils flared in a gentle face.

An udder indicated, promise
of milk, promise of young.

A creature from a creature,
honoured with ochre,

in a bell-shaped pit buried
with care, deliberately broken.

So she survived, so she continues
to walk warily forward,

mouth open at a tender skew –
as if to take the air, as if to say

We keep going, though we are
all in some way wounded.

Milkweed

for Carole Herrle

Up in the air almost before your envelope was opened,
the seedheads – as if possessed of motive power.
They'd cling to my fingers but not be caught.

Magic Milkweed you'd written. You must have known
how they'd lift and drift through the room, sunlight
silvering their silk. If you meant a blessing, I was blessed.

I thought of rich runnels of milk sprung from rock
at a god's command; of Vermeer's Cook, from a jug
never-empty to a bowl never-filled her steady pour;

of sap and nectar the seeds give rise to, fuel
for miles on miles of butterflies making their way
from Mexico to Canada to Mexico;

of that lava tunnel, vicious, fire-spiked walls,
utter dark, blind crabs so small and white
in the spotlit pool, their one and only home.

As they went their own way I could almost hear
the seedheads' hunger, their itch for increase.
They wouldn't be caught. They wanted the earth.

A Far Cry

A swallow swerves across a dune
and veers out over the sea,
appears, disappears so quickly
it leaves an ache in your eyes,
an ache in your heart.

The open sky is an empty page
where the writ has never run,
and a poem is a far cry,
and it cannot hold you, though
it holds you, swallow, gone.

Mackerel

line no sooner down than taut
    shadow silvering into air
desperate fruit all wriggle
    and twitch snapped off
slapped in a plastic crate
    fading to layers of leaves
knives out guts chucked
    to an instant coven of gulls
heads scarfed whole
    sea a boil of snatch and scream
fillets home in a bucket
    fried in their own oil
all night my head full
    of saltwater skin sun
flesh feather beak bone
    so little between us

Port Hardy

(VANCOUVER ISLAND)

Since the copper and the army went
the town's got really small,
the young waitress is saying.
There's fishing, logging, tourists –
that's pretty much it.

We sit and eat and listen.
Beyond the large windows
the estuary shuffles its silks,
lavender, slate-grey, silver.

A man from lower down the States
passed through last summer,
he made the whole journey
on a single paddle raft,
heading to Prince Rupert and then back,
just him and a board and a paddle.
He was a castaway – Tom Hanks!

Hot light pools on the horizon.
Water's a deeper, darker blue,
rose-stippled, streaked and frosted
with shivers of breeze,
like the skin of the autumn salmon
which break the surface to hang
long, improbable moments in air.

I'd like to travel while I can, she says.
Europe maybe, I could sleep on trains,
I've heard people do that there.

Sun flames off the water,
reddens the room.

We're not allowed to serve alcohol,
I'm sorry, she says, in answer
to a couple just come in. The man glares.
His wife keeps her head down.
He mutters, pushes back his chair,
swears as he brushes past the waitress,
calling his wife after him.

I'm sorry, she says, just holding her smile,
out there on the floor,
framed against the enormous light.

Water and Stone

(NAMIBIA)

Zaris Mountains

Where, until it was shouldered off,
a sea kept adding to its mattress.

Where mud became a darkroom,
developed lasting impressions.

Ancient plates stacked up,
stained with strange remains.

A press where leaves and beings were stored,
until names could be found for them.

Zebra River Valley

A house-martin swimming
in the wide open pool
of a canyon.

On the cliff rim
where it was perched,
tiny white circles.

From the base of a cliff
to the quiver tree pinned
on its rim, how far?
A billion years, give or take.

The odd clatter,
as if somewhere

in the vast warren
of canyon and cliff

someone kept
dropping crockery.

The fresh face, when a stone is opened,
and the smell: fust of unentered church.

Simple fact of stone.
The given living room,
the end of light.

On whose closed book
someone's always writing
This can't be all.

≈

Zebra River

Dried up but everywhere its abandon,
the valley a hotel room the river left
in a hurry, stones it sucked and smoothed
spat out and scattered.

High in a side-valley a small seep,
a faint light under a door through which
the river might one day burst back in
and hurl itself down on its bed.

≈

Way up a canyon wall
a baboon. It shouts.
Echoes rattle down
the cliffs, settle
into visible silence

≈

Nothing had been touched,
handsaws and cleavers,
blades and scrapers
found where last left
on the floor of the cave –
as if those who used them
had just popped out,
would return any minute
to take up their tools,
blowing away
a half-million-year
dressing of dust.

We had taken shelter
under a flowering thorn
when a kudu danced past,
its horns like the first lyre,
just needing to be strung
to start the whole story.

Vogelfedersburg

Remnant of ground-down mountain,
broken open dome on the peneplain;

granite onion, skins peeled
by slow crowbars of moisture and air.

Grain by grain it goes, the reluctant rock,
a cupful of grulsh in a decade.

The base, cored by sand-strung wind,
offers an overhang, an outstretched wing.

Than the time taken to fashion that wing,
human history has lasted no longer.

⋍

The Burnt Mountain
was never in flames.
Its shales were baked,
the lake vegetation
exhaled.

In late evening light
the Mountain glows,
shining slopes of red
and purple oxides
by erosion exposed.

⋍

Strict laws dictate
that bodies that can't
form freely form
polygons, hence
these organ pipes,
dolerite squeezed

into bedrock,
cooled, contracted
columns of basalt,
deep, ordained as
the roots of music.

Twyfelfontein

It was where water entered the world,
hurrying its endless flocks out of stone.

But there were times water turned back,
the last few tails shrinking into cliff.

No one knew where it had gone to then.
Bird, animal, human, in this together.

In the spirit-shape of a chosen creature
a shaman would dream himself into rock,

drum his way down the empty aquifers,
find the flocks and try to coax their return.

Each drumbeat a halter placed gently
around a neck, he would lead the flocks

up towards the light, never looking back.

Three years of water
in Cinderella Valley,
after ten years of drought.

Beside a thin fall
a hammerskop has domed
an empty buzzard nest.

Like a wooden ball
it awaits a baboon's kick.
Water melts into grass.

Kunene River

Highest leaves burn in last light.
A blizzard of finches blows itself out.
At night the river becomes a hymn
sung by massed choirs of cicadas.
Dawn finds her back in her bed.

Ten minutes after sunset the waterhole
seethes with grouse no one sees arriving.
Shadow is scored by their piped cry –
Don't weep so Charlie, Don't weep so Charlie.
 Again and again they rush in. The water
their breasts soak up will be carried
to nests far out in the desert, will be
the only moisture their chicks receive.

Andean Cocks of the Rock

(ECUADOR)

Steep, cut-out paths lead us down
into a ravine, head-torches burning
in early morning dark. Eyes pricked
for the likely sight of a pygmy-owl.
Trying not to touch thorned trunks,
bullet ants, nettles with a horse's kick.

Down and down until we reach a platform,
its bamboo canopy all shoot and sprout.
We stare into dim, tangled abundance,
wait for the cocks to come to their lek.
You don't see but suddenly you hear,
a raucous, echoey, electric clamour
jetting and jerking through the silence.

With our optics, cameras, notebooks, guides,
our packed lunches waiting up above,
we sit. Sound is not what we came for
but for a moment it's as if it were –
to hear this voice not intended for us,
telling us something we might have known,
something we'd forgotten we'd forgotten.

We get a glimpse of the scarlet birds,
heads strangely flattened, almost faceless.
When we climb back up to daylight
the sound can still be heard, rising
from the ground, an ancient river
running under the notes we start to make.

Omar Tello's Family

On seven hectares of worn-out ground
they've made a refuge for rainforest,
for years going out in their spare time
to bring in seedlings from the clearances,
finding for each one the right soil,
letting them grow until crowns touch
and seal a roof to bring a forest into being.

Leaf-winged grasshoppers,
moths made of bark, glass butterflies;
stick-mimics, beetles dipped in liquid metal,
the spiders which rivet the ship …
And each year out of the blue
more insects come.

The town is surrounding them,
isolating the sanctuary they've created.
Quietly proud, quietly angry,
with a lighted lens Omar's daughter
lets us in on the teased-out roots,
the tiny flowers of the rescued orchids,
secured to the right trunk with wool.

Angel Paz Talks to the Birds

María. Cariňa.
María, Pequeňa.

He crouches on a path,
croons, whistles gently.

María. Cariňa.
María, Pequeňa.

At last something emerges,
coaxed from thick undergrowth,

climbing out of darkness
onto an open path.

Silent, solemn, cocked
right back on its legs.

Large, round, almost tailless.
Stands utterly still.

Golden, rusty-barred breast.
Sloe-grey shoulders.

A giant antpitta,
awkward in daylight

but there, charmed from
the shadow it inhabits,

somehow responding,
shiest, wariest bird,

to something
in Angel's voice.

It looks at the worms
he's placed on the path.

Eats one or two
but keeps its distance.

When it feels it's been there
long enough, it leaves.

Angel folds away his voice.
And whatever that voice

has allowed to emerge
inside, we too fold away.

Terma de Virgén

Everyone crowds
at the close of day
into the hot pool
under the waterfall,
a high thin fraying
from the great ridge
above the town,
floodlit, a white feather,
skinny, frisking tail
of a mountain horse.

Oldest to youngest
we crowd in together,
under the fall
our different wounds.
See us unclothed
as sun goes down,
in water's forgiveness
gently held.

Never to Run Out

(VANCOUVER ISLAND)

We didn't find Forest Woman,
nor Wild Man of the Woods,
we found only trees and rock,
greenblack water and sky.

I could list the fine detail:
wild rose, bunchberry, mountain everlasting,
swallowtail and black admiral,
dark-eyed junco and winter wren,

but what mattered was the wood
and the stone, the roots locked onto rock,
the cold, dark, giving water,
the ancient, dust-stained light,

the sun up there remote and near,
the glimpse of a moon's ghostflake
and the path running forward,
the way between the trees.

There was an agreement,
an understanding, a wanting
to go on and on and never stop,
as if the day might never end.

I could find a name
for the steepness and the shadow,
for the ache in my bones,
for all that's been lost and sometimes why

but there was only walking
and this endless appetite for more,
more wood, more stone, more water, more light,
for the path never to run out;

for distance which when reached
would open to become again distance.

Winter Solstice, Knockroe

Help me, says the sun.

Guide me over
the darkening grass.

Each blade resists.

Help me
reach these stones.

House me
this long night.

30th August 2013

i.m. Seamus Heaney

The sun was white, as though chidden of God –
an early morning out of Hardy.

When the mist lifted we found we could see,
down the road and into the distance,

how scraps of straw hung from hawthorn twigs
and shone in soft heaps at the verge –

as if not a trailer but you had passed
and even here shed light as you went

on your way, gratefully, into the earth.

Anniversary

I walk down through the glen
to the lake Joe and Eilis have made,
filled by the stream off the hill.

End of October –
in a leaf's slow burn and fall
the sense of a threshold.

I go to drop a late rose
on the water, to watch it steady
on the current and be swept away.

I don't come with a golden bough,
to encounter your shade.
I've no song to bring you back.

I strip and force myself in. The cold
that bites after one or two strokes –
that's what I'm after.

I want to be stopped in my tracks,
speechless, one big shudder.
To have to turn back

because I have to turn back.
I come stooped out of the water.
I remind myself of you.

Dispatch

I was left to cradle you
while our neighbour ran
for his wife, a nurse.

I prayed you'd not come to,
find yourself dying
in a stranger's arms.

Let not such loneliness
my going hence attend.

The Wood

I hadn't noticed the sound of the traffic
from the new road behind the wood
until one night you told me to listen.

I heard it then of course and found
I could see headlights, working their way
like a quiet army through the trees.

Somehow still, outside at night,
I don't notice until reminded,
though the traffic continues to run,

like the traffic outside that house
where I lay and waited for one car to slow,
its light on the ceiling to die.

Pumpkin

Sits on a rumpled bed of leaves,
red and round as a harvest moon,
round and ripe as Buddha's belly.

Baked all day in the sun's oven,
through a green pipe slurping
earth's liquid and mineral.

Here it begins and here it ends.
Nothing but pumpkin,
not a leg to stand on

but the whole world its sure support.
A fat, firm, featureless sphere.
From its skin all questions slide.

Doubtless

All day on hands and knees,
it happened to be autumn,
could have been any season.
I was pulling out old bulbs,
hands joyous with mud.

Through puddle in the next field
a horse sploshed and sucked –
a rook called, a rag of mist
snagged on a pine and doubt
left me on my own a while.

Sometimes a thing is what it is,
not an excuse for another thing.
And if I felt I was getting close
to somewhere else, I knew
it was not a place to be reached.

What mattered was appetite.
The shadows that gathered
were shadows of what was there.
Sun and moon both in the sky,
with me all of the way.

Glossy Ibis

Mussel-black, broad, fingered wings
barely moving to lift the birds
high against a bright winter sky.

Twenty of them, two broken lines,
heading out to sea then turning back,
drifting down to the flooded race track.

When I look at something beautiful,
said Coleridge, *it seems as if I were*
on the brink of a fruition still denied –

as if vision were an appetite.
Or, taken for its own sweet sake, flight.

Walking

after Nazim Hikmet

Walking round the sandhills.

Walking round the sandhills,
every single day.

Walking round the sandhills,
every single day,
first light until last.

Walking round the sandhills,
every single day,
first light until last,
people and their dogs.

Walking round the sandhills,
every single day,
first light until last,
people and their dogs,
every kind of person,
every kind of dog.

Walking round the sandhills,
every single day,
first light until last,
people and their dogs,
every kind of person,
every kind of dog,
the waves breaking white.

Walking round the sandhills,
every single day,
first light until last,
people and their dogs,
every kind of person,
every kind of dog,
the waves breaking white,
the air always fresh.

The dogs, in time, will go,
in time people will go too.
One day the sandhills will go.
The waves and the sea will go,
days will go and air will go,
and at last the sun will go

and that's why every single day,
first light until last,
people and their dogs,
every kind of person,
every kind of dog,
are walking round the sandhills,
the waves breaking white,
the air always fresh.

2

*We lack the wings to fly, but will always
have the strength to fall.*
— Paul Claudel

After the Fall

What came from my mouth
was not word but bawl –
as I think now
of pain of course,
but also triumph –
Still here! Still here!

I made arrangements.
I knew I'd be saved.
All I could do then
was look and listen.
A wren threading heather.
A pipit's measured bounds.

The stream carried on,
sliding over sills,
speeding as it dropped,
calming down in pools.
The constant chatter
and good cheer,

the voice it gives
to rock's enormous reserve.
No blame for the place.
No blame for myself.
I lay there open
as a daisy,

almost resenting
the helicopter,
the rescue it brought,
the helping hands

come to lift me from
this strange, broken grace.

Stretchers

1.

Not on a stretcher
lowered through a roof
into a healer's house,
but on a stretcher
lifted from the ground
to a safe house in sky.

2.

In A & E strapped flat
and on my own so long
I began to believe
the ceiling was the floor.
I hung over space,
only straps to stop
my falling again –
then your face,
through the gulf I looked
down on towards me
looking down.

X-Ray

Grace of the neck's bearing, its fluent stoop,
how it holds like a spring the skull's bowl:
a flower stalk, a thin leaning tower
whose each storey floats on a bed of air.

'We must look after you most carefully,'
said the doctor. He was talking to you,
not me. Look at the crack and the chip.
Hard but helpless bone, awful to gaze upon.

Lifted from the dim physical world, lit,
how you hate this close scrutiny,
this numbering, this public discussion.
My flesh cringes on you, rag and shadow –

and you rise and shine. Gingerly I edge
along the corridors, hiding, haunted by
the most gentle swan: nerve-feathered bird,
already mending, without a word.

Gravity

We all come
through the gate into your field
    and so gently
you keep us in place we forget,
    your touch unfelt.

Each day your weight takes
    an inch, each night
we rise slowly back to size.
    Pressed down
our heads open up to heavens.

    When I fell I knew
this was not a fall, it was you
    taking hold of me,
speeding me, rolling me over,
    I felt your grab

for the first time, push or pull
    I don't know which,
in those split seconds it seemed
    that mountain,
very earth and sky had turned

    against me, were
beating me up – but it was only
    your ancient will,
doing what it does, making
    light of everything.

Shadow (2)

It followed me on the grassy path
through the sunlit trees,
over the stone wall
and out onto the open hillside;

it stood with me
under the bridal hawthorns,
went along with song of the stream;

it sat with me as I drank my tea,
chopped and changed on heather and bilberry,
fell behind on the steepening slopes,
flowed in and out of the black gullies;

it found me at the foot of the cliff,
settled down there beside me,
content to mimic my small movements;

it drew my arm to the ground,
glad that this could still happen,
glad that its exact likeness would not
from the world of light be gone forever.

Aspen Collar

Aspen: sound and silver of leaves in light.
Why name this collar after such a tree?

Unlovely brace of plastic and padding,
velcroed tight to keep my head held high.

The constant close companionship,
the point-of-view imposed, the smell –

I couldn't wait to have you taken off.
Soon it seemed I ended at you,

surprised at night to find my face
above you in the mirror, an afterthought.

All day you'd held it on display,
saddled with the one story to tell.

Time and again assured of my luck,
my lips agreed. No secrets from you.

Your tight grip always allowed for doubt.
The more I wore you the less able my skin

to keep the inside in. Not, I knew,
my bones you held together, but me.

At last they took you off. I found my head
in my hands, telling a different story.

Break-in

It wasn't as if there was
a broken window-pane,
rain and leaves on a carpet,
a small table knocked over.

Wasn't as if you reached
for your wallet and found
it gone – it was more
one day you felt

something was missing,
you couldn't say what,
but you felt its absence,
began to ask around.

And all those you asked
wanted to help, as if
they all had some idea
what was missing.

And some said Yes,
they had seen it –
but what they described
seemed far from certain.

And so time went by,
never quite rightly.
And if it were found,
if it said *Here*, if it said

Hungry, if it said *Help Me,*
what have you to give
beyond your looking,
beyond your life of loss?

Things

So bright in the stream shone the stone
I couldn't resist lifting it out,
though I knew it would fade as it dried.

'It's the day you stop picking them,
that day you give up,' someone said.
Could I keep it lit in a glass of water?

'You should have left it where it was,'
said someone else. 'Enjoy it, move on.'
Everything we treasure will be lost.

The stream's luminous room. I had tried
to take from it what couldn't be taken.
My house is full of such shortcoming.

There is a room I have never entered.
Against the chance I ever will
grows the pile of things at its door.

Chagall's *The Lovers of Vence*

Her hair is moon-yellow, her face
the tender green of the fields.

His hair burns like the sun
setting above the small hill village.

They share a bunch of blue flowers.
There are trees blue as the flowers.

Though he, it seems, is dressed,
only flowers cover her breasts.

She bought the print and carefully
for his birthday glued it to a board.

And all he could see was the tiny crease
she hadn't quite managed to flatten.

At the Table

Low sun through the window,
shadow-play on the walls,
sway of twigs and leaves,
different in their darks.
One shape behind another
like water on the walls,
water stacked against water,
never still, never touching.

Treens my mother left me,
her bowl of wooden eggs,
the red Venetian jug.
Oak coffer, centuries old,
where my father's father
left out his prescriptions.
A kind man I never met.

Painting of a chough.
Of an announcing angel.
A needle mounted in wax,
veiled in gauze and framed.
Shadow on the dining table,
solid as the coffer.

A forest of empty bottles,
winestains, guttered candles.
Shadow over them all,
shapes that sorrow makes
when shape itself breaks.

Bindweed

I loved to pinch the base to see
the white gramophone horn pop out
and swing upside down as it fell.

You'll never get rid of it, he said.
*You pull it up but there's always
a little bit left to grow again.*

It's true. No matter how I try
I can't get to the start of it.
I feel it climb and twine around

my ribs, coming into flower
and broadcasting
its silent white music through me,

over and over again.

Morning

Always there, morning
and the lit distance.

Some days dull as lead.
Once even snow. Maybe

nothing there but fog.
But distance, always.

Even the fog just a veil
on its face, a modesty.

Horseshoe of the bay –
still there. Still there

sandhill, headland, sky.
Boats or not out at sea.

Usual huddle of gulls.
Usual roads and houses.

Loyal morning,
on which you can feast

your eyes but not feed;
far distance, where

you have always felt
closer to home. And

always this invitation
to speak your grief,

always this chance
to answer back,

always this refusal.

My Father's Budgerigars

I didn't know they were parrots,
never dreamt they belonged
to that gaudy, noisy family.

In their homemade wooden cages
with their millet-stalks, mirrors and bells,
I didn't even think of them as birds.

They were like boys with the faces
of old men – boys somehow
transformed and caged.

Legs shrunk and scaly,
wings just the means to shift
from perch to perch.

No surprise to learn that the word *Budgerigar*
contains a word for *Good* –
that the name might mean *Good Boy.*

On the Road

A thrush with no head.
An empty packet of Silk Cut
labelled 'Fumar Mata'.

20 Wild Woodbines for the Vicar,
we learnt to say at the shop.
I sense you at my heels.

I remember your head
under a towel,
inhaling Friar's Balsam.

'Una muerta lente y dolorosa'.
At a young age.
But not from cigarettes.

The bite of dinner
you managed at Christmas,
only to sick it up.

My mother ringing early,
having waited
until we might be awake.

Just before dawn, in his sleep.
He just stopped breathing,
gradually. That was all.

I sat with him
until the dawn came.
Then I went for a walk.

When I returned
I washed and dressed him.
I wasn't afraid, at all.

That quiet room,
and the gift of quiet
you gave each other.

I sense you at my heels,
a man after
my own heart.

The gift of quiet.
A quiet I'm covered in,
a quiet I break

to tell the difference
between us. To make
that difference.

The Garden

There you stand,
one foot on the spade.
It is nearly evening
and it will never be done.

Though gone so long
it is all so familiar.
Perhaps in dream
I make my visits.

I am older now
than you ever were
and you will always
be older than me.

What do you want?
I want you
to disown me.

Why am I still here?
You are digging down
for my tears.

Facebook

For you to come again like this –
Sue's wedding, forty years ago,
a photo posted by a cousin.

Brown suit, pipe, glass of wine.
In the background your shed,
the clutter you'd get round to.

I sit at the screen, unseen.
I might be what you wanted
me to be, and I might not.

Either way, I've come to believe
you would click on *Like*.
And how should I respond?

Happy. Sad. Angry. Confused.
No click for *Take my hand.*
Nothing to click for *Hold me.*

Celandine

It dawned on me from the roadside,
simple, goodhearted, yellow daisy,
set in a surrender of leaves,
mild-marbled, almost heart-shaped.

Huge winds were ripping into the trees,
a thrush was singing, near but remote,
a cold-voiced clock striking short psalms,
beseechment, lament, into the wind.

Someone was holding my hand. A voice said
The green swallow, the first of spring,
Celandine, from the Greek for swallow, Chelidon.
And here's another word for you to savour:
Chelidonias, a swallow-bearing wind.

The Lane

What I liked most about those healing walks
was not just what we'd take in on the way:
the horse straying over, pulling up short,
never quite meeting us face to face;
the hare that crossed our path, strange contraption,
always on the look-out for its one missing part;
the deep cool of the concrete water trough
under the oak tree, the seven giddying calves.

No, best was when we turned on our heels.
To turn was to look into the old valley,
worn hills, blue hedge and down there our house;
was to know we could walk along the track,
through the farm, down the shit-creamy lane
and let ourselves in through the gate.
It was open to us always to return.
You must have felt it too: each time we turned,
that's where you reached for, took my hand.

Alfie

Buried in his favourite cardigan,
its arms crossed to hold him in our heads.
A paw reaching up to touch a face.
A sprig of the grass he loved to tunnel.
A feather of the magpie he never caught.

He was a spirit sent to help you,
to carry you through those dark days.
He wasn't. He was a kitten dumped
on a farm, rescued from a dog's mouth.
Alone, he hid far out of harm's way.

Taken to the cattery on a wild night
he broke out of his basket and fled
deep into a thicket of bramble.
I called for hours until he came, called
as if our lives too depended on it.

His trust in the nine lives given to him
was never broken, hurt as he'd been.
Delight used up a few of those lives –
sheer joy of following eye, nose and ear.
The early morning car he didn't survive.

What has happened, he would teach us,
has happened. There will be times to hide,
there will be times to race through grass
and leap high into a yew tree,
not the slightest doubt it will hold you.

Oak

for Aoine Landweer-Cooke

Because it leans across the field like a farmer at a gate.
Because it has no face, no front, no back.
Because it lifts a soft coat of ferns into the air.
Because its trunk is hard as stone.
Because in winter the high tracery of twigs
holds and frames many hundred fragments of sky.
Because it is a window not a mirror.
Because new trunks break from it
and try to grow upright and it does not mind.
Because if one way is blocked it will grow in another.
Because it does not judge.
Because a great fountain rises inside it
and this is all the work of its leaves
and no one knows quite how they do it.
Because each leaf is so small and short-lived.
Because its feet go deep into the earth
and so much of its life goes unseen.
Because one day it will fall.
Because here a man spoke up
for the boy he had once been.
Because its branches cannot help but corkscrew.
Because its twigs twist and fly off into space.
Because it does resemble a wild-headed dancer.

Bee Orchids

He'd been rowed
across the Rinnashark
to see them one last time
before he died.

The photo of his hand
cupped round a flower,
a letting go
and a leaving be.

So hard to find them
in the kidney vetch,
in the marram grass
and the dead marram grass.

I found three, one inside,
two outside the dune.
On that dark evening
I took them as a sign.

Making
the strange meanings
you make
when you're alone.

But the orchids –
their motley faces,
bright pink tricorn,
snaily horns.

So grave and so silly.
They stared me down.